AD and ML King

AD and ML King

Two Brothers who Dared to Dream

By Naomi Ruth Barber King

Foreword by Dr. Babs Onabanjo

AuthorHouse™ LLC
1663 Liberty Drive
Bloomington, IN 47403
www.authorhouse.com
Phone: 1-800-839-8640

© 2014 Naomi Ruth Barber King. All rights reserved.

No part of this book may be reproduced, stored in a retrieval system, or transmitted by any means without the written permission of the author.

Selected Photos courtesy of Dr. Christine King Farris and The AD King Foundation

Published by AuthorHouse   06/16/2014

ISBN: 978-1-4969-1916-8 (sc)
ISBN: 978-1-4969-1915-1 (e)

Any people depicted in stock imagery provided by Thinkstock are models, and such images are being used for illustrative purposes only. Certain stock imagery © Thinkstock.

This book is printed on acid-free paper.

Because of the dynamic nature of the Internet, any web addresses or links contained in this book may have changed since publication and may no longer be valid. The views expressed in this work are solely those of the author and do not necessarily reflect the views of the publisher, and the publisher hereby disclaims any responsibility for them.

Dr. Martin Luther King, Jr. and Rev. Alfred Daniel Williams King
Two Brothers who Dared to Dream

"Here comes the dreamer!" they said. "Come on, let's kill him and throw him into one of these cisterns. We can tell our father, 'A wild animal has eaten him.' Then we'll see what becomes of his dreams!" Genesis 37: 19-20

"For God so loved the world, that He gave His only begotten Son (Jesus Christ); so that whosoever believes on Him shall not perish, but shall have everlasting life; For God did not send His Son into the world to condemn the world; but that the world through Him might be saved." John 3:16-17

Table of Contents

Dedication xi
Acknowledgements xiii
Foreword xvii
Introduction xxiii

A Humble Beginning 1
My Boaz 11
A Legacy of Love 17
Sons of Thunder 21
Brothers in the Struggle: Precious Memories............. 39

Afterword 55
About the Author 63
Appendix 69
Williams-King Family Tree 75
Poetry - For Generations To Come 76

Dedication

"This book is dedicated to people! I love people! I especially love children- born innocent! Hatred is taught! …In the name of Sweet Jesus, our Savior – in the name of Love… In my head, heart and eyes – Love has no color! Blessings…"

Naomi Ruth Barber King

Acknowledgements

This book is first dedicated to Father God, Lord Jesus and Holy Spirit with deepest devotion and gratitude. Also, to the entire Williams- King Family, my children, grandchildren and great-grandchildren; to all the foot-soldiers of the Civil Rights Movement who fought so bravely and tirelessly; to Dr. Babs Onabanjo, President of the AD King Foundation; Dr. Alveda King and Rev. Derek Barber King; to my belated husband and all my dearly departed children and all family members; and to all who have worked to make this book possible; thank you and God bless you. We dedicate this ballad of love to the beloved community, and most importantly, to God Almighty be the honor, praise and glory."

-Mrs. Naomi Ruth Barber King

"Man proposes but God disposes."
-Mrs. Naomi Ruth Barber King

"We have had so many troubles tonight but if you're going to kill someone then kill me. But stand up for your right, stand up for justice, stand up for equality, stand up for peace and freedom but with non-violence."

-Rev. Alfred Daniel King, May 11, 1963

Foreword

The Civil Rights Movement led by Dr. Martin Luther King Jr. would not be complete without the undeniable contributions and unfettered or rather unconditional support of the little-known icon in his own right and brother to the dreamer Rev. A D Williams King. I was moved and compelled to bring this story into the limelight because it has been missing in action by commission, design or omission for so long. As Dr. King would say that justice delayed is justice denied.

Rev A D King deserves a place in the history of the Civil Rights Movement. Rev A D King was involved in the civil rights movement as much as his brother, MLK Jr. Underlying it all is the lack of recognition of the role of Rev A D king in the movement and the deliberate attempt to undermine his contributions.

However, Mrs. Naomi Ruth Baber King in writing this book is determined to bring into perpetual existence the truth about the role of her husband, Rev A D Williams King in the civil rights movement. Without the three laws enacted by the Congress in the sixties, in which A D King was directly involved, it would have been impossible to have elected an African-American as the president of the United States of America.

Mrs. Naomi King adequately narrates the role of Rev A D King and his contribution to the Civil rights movement, the sacrifices, the bombing of their house in Birmingham (Ensley), the bombing of their church in Louisville, Kentucky, the threats and eventually the mysterious death of Rev. A D Williams King in Atlanta Georgia, a little over one year after the assassination of Dr. Martin Luther King on July 21, 1969.

As we remember, celebrate and honor Dr. Martin Luther King and all the foot soldiers, we should always remember, Rev A D King, the only blood brother to the dreamer, the confidant of the dreamer and the strategist of the movement who supported his brother until death.

During the course of my research, I uncovered many interesting, little-known insights about the Civil Rights Movement, its participants and the significant role of Rev A D King. I was compelled to do something about it. With Mrs. Naomi King and my team, we decided to tell a very honest and more complete story of the important moments in American history by developing a documentary entitled "Behold The Dream: Brother To The Dreamer", which was first premiered at the King Center in 2009. The completed documentary was premiered at Morehouse College in Atlanta in 2010 with almost Two Thousand in attendance.

Many civic-minded leaders throughout the country have embraced our vision and committed to our endeavor, including former US Ambassador Andrew Young, Rev. Dr. Joseph Lowery, Rev Billy Kyles, Legendary Dick Gregory, Rev Willie Bolden, Rev. Dr. C.T. Vivian, Honorable John Lewis, Rev Dr. Otis Moss, Jr., Senator Georgia Powers,

Rev Dr. Charles Steel Jr, Joe Beasley, Rev Dr. Cameron Alexander, Rev. Joseph Boone and many others.

In order to continue the work of Rev A D King, Mrs. Naomi King and I established The A D King Foundation to preserve the legacy of Rev. A D Williams King. The mission of the organization is to promote youth empowerment and to embrace non-violent social change strategies as a way of life.

Mrs. Naomi King is a woman of grace and distinction, and she is known as a butterfly queen. Like the butterfly, Mrs. King brings beauty and joy to everyone around her. She is a woman of great intellect, full of love and compassion in spite of all she has gone through. Naomi Ruth Barber King has received several awards: Sclc Rosa Park Freedom Award 2008, Hope Worldwide Living legend Award 2009, History Markers 2010, Legacy Ladies' Tea Award 2011, Bimini Peace Retreat 2013, Presidential National Volunteer Award 2013, The Life Principled Award 2014 and many others.

Finally, this is the love story of an extra-ordinary woman of courage, a living legend in her own right, committed to unveiling the truth about her beloved husband, after many years of perseverance, toils and snares, equipped with the unconditional love of God and the power of forgiveness. This is the story of two brothers as eloquently stated by Rev Kyles that AD's legacy will open doors that people can look into and see the life and times of these brothers, not like Cain and Abel, but like ML and AD.

Thank you, Mrs. Naomi King for sharing your courage, tenacity, grace, love and fortitude in preserving the family's legacy and the contributions of your beloved husband to the civil rights movement. We all look forward to your next book, "When Brothers Pray: AD & ML King," which will be devoted to "Generation Z;" the youth of the "Beloved Community."

Dr. Babs Onabanjo.
President and CEO, The A D King Foundation.
www.adkingfoundation.com www.adkingfoundation.ning.com

AD King

Rev. Dr. Alfred Daniel Williams King, brother to Rev. Martin Luther King Jr., was one of the main strategists behind several Civil Rights campaigns. Rev. A. D. King's house was bombed in Birmingham, May 11, 1963 as a result of his activism in Ensley and Birmingham Alabama. According to records of the SCLC archive at the King Center: " It is widely held that the Birmingham demonstrations led directly to the passage of the Civil Rights Act of 1964 and that the Selma Campaign compelled the U.S. Congress to enact the Voting Rights Act of 1965." Rev. A.D. King led the Open Housing Campaign in Louisville Kentucky, which became a national law The Open Housing Act - 1968. Both of my brothers paid the ultimate price for their role in the Civil Rights Movement...Dr. Christine King-Farris.

www.adkingfoundation.com

Lo, children are an heritage of the Lord: and the fruit of the womb is his reward. As arrows are in the hand of a mighty man; so are children of the youth. Happy is the man that hath his quiver full of them: they shall not be ashamed, but they shall speak with the enemies in the gate. (Psalms 127:3-5 KJV)

Introduction

I came into the King family when I married my late husband, Reverend Alfred Daniel Williams King, I. Because he lived in the shadow of his very famous brother, Dr. Martin Luther King, Jr., many people don't know that my husband was a hero in his own right. AD's life mirrored ML's in many ways. Firebombs devastated the Birmingham, Alabama house where we lived with our five children. Later, during our ministry in Louisville, where AD spearheaded demonstrations for open housing, the chapel at our church, Zion, was bombed. AD was a major strategist and organizer for the Movement, and he is often called a giant of a man.

People often ask me if my husband participated in the marches and demonstrations with his brother. When I tell them that AD was at almost every march and demonstration led by his brother, the next question is invariably, "Why don't we ever see him? There are not many pictures and historical accounts. Many people don't even know there was an AD King."

Perhaps the answer lies in the very character and nature of my husband. AD and ML were always very close, even from their earliest childhood days. ML was always more staid, studious and philosophical. AD was more outgoing, charismatic, and bold. Yet the two always stood up for each other. The two brothers remained close and fierce in their love and loyalty to each other until the very end. Now they are in Heaven together, a beautiful conclusion to their life on earth.

In the Movement, ML relied heavily on AD for unconditional support, advice and his organizational skills. Understanding his supportive role with his brother as the focal point, AD had no desire to compete. He accepted his role of providing support, a modern day Aaron to Moses; or a Bobby Kennedy to John Kennedy; and he remained unwavering in his love and support of his brother. Although he was the younger, he also served as a "protector" for his "big brother."

I often noticed that while most of those in ML's inner circle often pushed to have the most prominent seats and positions next to ML, AD was often pushed into the background by those more aggressive in seeking positions. AD was so secure in his relationship with his brother, and with his calling from God, that he often worked unceasingly and effectively in the light of God that surrounded him and his brother.

In many instances, truly in most, I was in the background and on the sidelines, yet I was there. As the wife of a major participant of a most significant part of history, I remember many events.

AD and I were married for nineteen years. It often seems as if those short years spanned many lifetimes. This is our story, of living links in "The King Family Legacy".

Our lives have been stormy, God-inspired, romantic and often adventurous. My life with AD King is at the heart of this book. I am forever grateful to God for giving me to this very special man, Reverend Alfred Daniel Williams King, I. He will be forever treasured in my heart of hearts. The good Lord gives, and receives back unto His own. To God be the glory, the honor, and the praise.

The Lord had said to Abram, "Leave your native country, your relatives, and your father's family, and go to the land that I will show you. I will make you into a great nation. I will bless you and make you famous, and you will be a blessing to others. I will bless those who bless you and curse those who treat you with contempt. All the families on earth will be blessed through you." (Genesis 12:1-3 NLT)

A Humble Beginning

The fabric of any family is woven with many threads. There is laughter, there is pain, there is romance, and there is tragedy. Such is the story of the life of the King family. For many people, the King family is only ML (Martin), his widow (Coretta) and their four children. This is because history and the public eye ever seek celebrities. In reality, the King family is so much more than ML's branch.

For many years, the vibrant, creative members of our family have lived in ML's shadow. Yet, each of us, in our own way, has shared and experienced the pain and the triumphs of the legacy for which ML is remembered. So often, we are asked, "How did you do it? Did the same things happen to you as happened to Dr. King and his family?" The answer is unequivocally, yes! We were threatened and harassed. We lived in the center of the storm. How did we do it? We had faith in God! When others would have fainted, we prayed. Like the song, "We Shall Overcome" says, "God is on our side, we are not afraid, the Lord will see us through." And truly, God has always been with us. We are a family of faith. The manifesto of the Civil Rights Movement and the lasting foundation of our family stand upon the foundation of Jesus Christ; our hope is built upon nothing less. History sometimes fails to emphasize the importance of our faith during our times.

The magical, mystical "King Legacy" of our times started with the bloodlines of Martin Sr. and his wife,

Alberta. They had three living children. I have known and loved each of them as my family, and AD as my husband.

My husband, Rev. Alfred Daniel King (AD) was born on July 30, 1930. He was the third of three siblings; his brother and closest friend, Rev. Dr. Martin Luther King, Jr. (ML) was born on January 15, 1929. Their sister, Willie Christine King Farris was the firstborn of the trio. While ML became the most famous member of the King legacy, AD and ML were indeed "brothers in the struggle."

Both brothers and their sister were born to happy and blessed parents; Daddy King and Mama King. They lived in a lovely home in Atlanta, GA. The house is still there on Auburn Avenue and is now historically referred to as the "Birth Home".

ML was named after his father, Rev. Martin Luther King, Sr., who was also known as Daddy King. AD was named in honor of his mother's grandfather, Dr. Adam Daniel Williams. These great men – father and grandfather – influenced more than just the names of their offspring; their wisdom helped to shape their dreams.

The family was very close as the children were growing up on Auburn Avenue. The brothers were practically inseparable. They were each other's closest friend. They often didn't even call each other AD and ML. They often called each other "Brother."

Daddy King and Mama King would often listen to them practicing on Saturdays to learn their father's preaching style. Once "Dad" realized that they weren't making fun of his "whooping," he enjoyed listening to his sons preach as they grew in the Word of God. Daddy King would often say how gifted both of his sons were. Yet they each had their own unique and effective style. Daddy King would often say, "Thank God for my sons, they are truly a gift from God."

ML loved reading and writing, but AD loved to sing and play the violin and other musical instruments. All three children experienced the benefits of private piano lessons in their home. Mama King was an organist and the music director at Ebenezer Baptist during her years as first lady.

Daddy King, AD and ML often sang what Daddy King called "ditties" when they preached. These short songs would be "snatches" of their favorite hymns, anthems and Negro Spirituals. This style of singing/preaching is a common practice among gospel preachers. Back then, if the musicians couldn't pick up the King preachers' tunes, they sang a cappella in their rich low tenor to baritone voices. They had family "tessitura," that unique sound that let you know a King was singing. Music was a family gift from God through Mama King.

Mama King was very spiritual; yet she was very practical. She had a sense of humor, a fine sense for the arts, and a special touch for music. The Bible has a lot to say about music, song, dance, worship and praise.

```
Praise the Lord, for the Lord is good; celebrate his lovely
name with music. (Psalms 135:3 NLT)
```

Mama King was one to support and produce wonderful concerts and plays. As a result, music has always been regarded as vital; ever present at the heart of the worship and recreation in the lively King family households.

AD was always protective of ML. As the youngest of the three, AD was a little more playful and was also physically stronger than his "big brother." He was well known in the neighborhood as a tough young boy who would protect his brother at all costs. He would never allow the bullying and unfounded hatred of others to distract him and his brother from their greater goals. AD was courageous and as fearless as a lion.

In those days, their parents always taught them to tell the truth however, none of the King children were ever "tattlers;" they didn't "rat" on each other and were very loyal to each other. Nevertheless, they generally admitted their faults. Sometimes they were punished, yet loving instruction tended to be the order of the day in their lives. Even though I didn't meet AD until he was a youth, and wasn't there when he was a young boy growing up, I know that he came from a very loving home. This sure foundation, the love of his parents and family, and the love of my Mother Bessie and above all the Love of God was the basis and model for us when we started to build our own family unit.

For the most part, the King children were obedient and respectful to the authority of their elders. Daddy and Mama King would see to it that the children read the Bible every day. At the dinner table, they would recite and dialogue with their parents about the true meaning of the verses they read.

Daddy King instilled discipline and was very autocratic; whatever decision he made was final. The children dared not to disobey him, but he allowed them to express their views and talk about anything with him. For example, after a news report or a Bible lesson, Dad would often ask, "ML, AD, what do you have to say?"

As you can see if you ever visit the King Family Birth Home in Atlanta, there is a dining room there where the young King family ate together, prayed together, exchanged ideas, sang and worshipped together. They were people of faith. So obedient and loving…

This is a family that I love so much and will forever cherish. The memories endured, the hope of a better tomorrow lingers on with abiding faith in God and the promises of tomorrow. Through God's divine purpose emerged the King Family legacy; a love for others, compassion and a deep sense of serving humanity.

Again, although I didn't know AD or his family back then, there are priceless historical moments to be found by visiting history books and historical sites. Actually, one of our grandchildren portrayed ML in a stage play "The Boy King," and he portrayed his grandfather AD in the television version. This remains his contribution to the history of our family.

It is important to know your history, where you came from, so you will always know where you are going. For me, the most important thing is to know this: "Always know who you are, and "Whose" you are." Knowing that I belong to Jesus and that Jesus loves me and belongs to me carries me through life's greatest challenges and greatest blessings.

And there have always been challenges, highs and lows in our family. Even though the world was in turmoil during those days, when they were growing up, I believe that the King children of their generation had a "normal" childhood. Yet they were deeply aware that there was a destiny, a prophetic calling looming over their futures. As we can see from these memories of their childhood, AD and ML were heavily influenced by their father, Rev. Martin Luther King, Sr., as well as their mother, Alberta Williams King (Mama King). Daddy King and Mama King had "freedom in their blood." Daddy King's lineage stemmed back to Ireland, where his grandfather Nathan Branham King boarded a ship to America to seek a better life for his family. Mama King's lineage stemmed from Africa.

During his lifetime, Mama King's grandfather, Willis Williams, was a respected "slave preacher" who preached to Blacks and Whites alike. Yes, freedom ran deep in the Williams-King bloodline. It still pulses throughout the legacy today. This family, born of Irish immigrants and former slaves, had a humble beginning. The Williams-King bloodline, a blend of African and Irish legacy is evidence of the truth of the scripture:

"And hath made of one blood all nations of men for to dwell on all the face of the earth, and hath determined the times before appointed, and the bounds of their habitation…" Acts 17:26

This foundational understanding, that there is only one human race, created of "one blood," and not separate races would become the basis of the family quest to embrace "The Beloved Community." Even as young boys, AD and ML were on the verge of discovering that there was destiny ahead that they had yet to imagine or dream.

As they were growing up, ML was the most serious of the three children. He enjoyed reading and meditating, contemplating the problems of the world and how to solve them. Early in life, the siblings encountered the effects of racism when traveling with their parents through segregated stores and establishments to do business. Daddy King was an activist in his own right, and Mama King's father had been an activist. Their children learned firsthand that they didn't have to accept treatment as second-class citizens.

AD had a sharp mind for organization, and from his youth, was interested in business. He was in pursuit of business strategies even as a youth when his natural charm and cheerful personality endeared him to potential clients. Some still smile and tease about how at church AD would open the doors for the ladies, and they were so impressed with his chivalrous conduct, that they would give him quarters as he escorted them down the stairs and across the street. Then they would thank him, pat his back or pull his ear.

Like Moses with his brother Aaron, ML and AD grew up to turn the world upside down with their revolutionary ideas. Some people say that their story also reminds them of the Kennedy brothers in that they worked so closely to try and build a better world.

With the help of God, and bolstered by the strength of so many foot soldiers, known and unknown, of the Civil Rights Movement, they were brothers in the struggle. AD and ML were at the forefront of one of the most powerful Civil Rights battles the world has ever known.

And Ruth said, Entreat me not to leave thee, or to return from following after thee: for whither thou goest, I will go; and where thou lodgest, I will lodge: thy people shall be my people, and thy God my God: (Ruth 1:16 KJV)

"Yes, I know," Boaz replied. "But I also know about everything you have done for your mother-in-law since the death of your husband. I have heard how you left your father and mother and your own land to live here among complete strangers. (Ruth 2:11 NLT)

My Boaz

I was born in Dothan, Alabama. My mother and I moved to Atlanta to live with her brother in the mid-1930s. In Atlanta, we moved across the tracks to Mechanicsville. The Kings were an affluent, middle-class family. My mother, Bessie Barber, married Mr. Bailey. Mama told me that my natural father was a Native American, part Cherokee. I never knew my natural father.

As young people, AD and I courted pretty much according to the customs of the day. There was no "dating" as it is called today. He was always very attentive and considerate of me, even to the point of showering me with gifts when his family would allow it. Having a sister his only sister, and his own "Mother Dear," AD knew how to treat women.

When I was sixteen years old, AD sponsored my first major social event. He gave me a "sweet sixteen party" at their family home. The elegant environment and the sense of family prepared me for the years to come. AD was my knight in shining armor. I was his "virgin princess." Today, chastity is almost unheard of. In those days, it was regarded as something special, to hold yourself pure for that one special person with whom you would spend the rest of your life. AD would be that special man for me.

Yes, AD King was a charming youth and was very handsome. He was also a very gifted young man. He had a gift with spoken words and the manner of presentation.

He was an eloquent speaker with charisma and a great personality. He captivated everyone within his sphere with every word that he spoke.

We got along very well and AD was very protective of me. He was my very first best friend. I happened to be from a very small family and was the only child of my mother. My mother took me to church every Sunday at Ebenezer Baptist Church in Atlanta. It was a very important staple in our home. AD was the youngest son of our pastor, Rev. Martin Luther King, Sr. and his beloved wife, Mrs. Alberta Williams King. God, in His infinite mercy, sent us to Ebenezer Baptist Church, where Daddy King was the "father" of his congregation. What has always been remarkable to me was that in his church, Daddy King treated everyone as equals. We found a home and a family in the congregation of the saints.

In those days, Daddy King was the famous "King." Having followed in the footsteps of his late father-in-law, Reverend Adam Daniel Williams, Daddy King was a fiery preacher and civil rights advocate in his own right.

My mother, Mrs. Bessie Barber and I were grateful members of Ebenezer. In those days, I guess you could say that I "caught AD's eye." Almost from the moment we met, AD would say that I was "the prettiest girl in the world," and that I would one day become his wife.

As time went on, AD and I were allowed to pursue a supervised "courtship." When I graduated from Booker

T. Washington High School in 1949, I chose to attend the prestigious Spelman College. It was everything I dreamed of as an educational experience. While attending Spelman, I fell deeply in love with my charismatic beau, AD King. Soon after, I became inspired by his dreams. We didn't know it, but the Civil Rights Movement was waiting to be born. ML was away in school. AD and I became serious. I left school to become his wife, and to start a family with my new husband. On June 17, 1950, I was the first to be married to one of the Williams-King siblings.

We married while we were young. Our first home was the family birth home where Christine, ML, and AD had been born years before. Daddy and Mama Alberta King had moved on to another home, and their first home was available for us to live in. We lived upstairs, and another family lived below.

At the King birth home, as it is known today, there were joys and challenges. Our son Derek broke his leg in the tree out back. Our precious Darlene suffered severe burns in an accident caused by a gaslight stove. Alveda cut her teeth there, and she cut her knee on the towering steel steps out back. She still has the scar today.

Of course, children of African-American descent were born in the black hospitals of that day. Years before, AD and his siblings had been born at the house, with Daddy King in tearful attendance. I always marvel at the compassion of Daddy King, who attended to his family with a tenderness that is rarely displayed in men. Over the years, as his family increased with marriages, Daddy King received us all with love and joy.

Dad's children were close to his heart, as were his grandchildren; and even his great-grandchildren. As daughters-in-law, Coretta and I felt little distinction. Dad often went shopping with Coretta or me. He often stopped by our homes to visit and eat and play with our children. He enjoyed dropping in on Coretta for hot, homemade vegetable soup and cornbread. Daddy King and Mama King were like that. Hot soup, cornbread, shopping trips, a father's love… it was all part of the plan. Their family grew in their garden of love because they watered it with faith and kindness. That old saying that "some people never meet a stranger," was true with them. As Naomi embraced Ruth as her daughter, and Ruth embraced Naomi as her mother, so it was with me in the King family legacy.

The wedding of Martin, Jr. and Coretta Scott King

"Three things will last forever --- Faith, Hope and Love --- and the greatest of these is Love… Love never fails. (I Corinthians 13: 8,13 NLT)

Rev. AD King and First Lady Mrs. Naomi King

A Legacy of Love

The greatest gift and greatest expression of the King Family Legacy has always been love. When I was pregnant with Alveda, Dad would come by our house every day with a bag of Lays potato chips, to "check and see how we were doing." The Lays plant was right around the corner, and Dad knew how much I enjoyed the chips.

I can remember when I first started calling him "Dad." Shortly after AD and I were married, we were at the "big house" for dinner. Mama King had everything laid out beautifully and the food was wonderful. I called Dad "Reverend King" at the table during this family gathering. He replied, "Baby. You call me Dad. I will be better to you than your own father would have been." Truly, Dr. Martin Luther King, Sr. was like a father to me, and better than the deceased biological father I never knew.

Yes, we had trials and joys. God was blessing us, and our family increased, and all five of our children—Alveda, Alfred, Derek, Darlene and Vernon—were born while we lived in that home. It would have been lovely for AD to live to see his grandchildren and great-grandchildren. Yet, God knows best.

I Corinthians 13

Though I speak with the tongues of men and of angels, and have not love, I am become as sounding brass, or a tinkling cymbal.

² And though I have the gift of prophecy, and understand all mysteries, and all knowledge; and though I have all faith, so that I could remove mountains, and have not love, I am nothing.

³ And though I bestow all my goods to feed the poor, and though I give my body to be burned, and have not love, it profiteth me nothing.

⁴ Love suffereth long, and is kind; love envieth not; love vaunteth not itself, is not puffed up,

⁵ Doth not behave itself unseemly, seeketh not her own, is not easily provoked, thinketh no evil;

⁶ Rejoiceth not in iniquity, but rejoiceth in the truth;

⁷ Beareth all things, believeth all things, hopeth all things, endureth all things.

⁸ Love never faileth: but whether there be prophecies, they shall fail; whether there be tongues, they shall cease; whether there be knowledge, it shall vanish away.

⁹ For we know in part, and we prophesy in part.

¹⁰ But when that which is perfect is come, then that which is in part shall be done away.

[11] When I was a child, I spake as a child, I understood as a child, I thought as a child: but when I became a man, I put away childish things.

[12] For now we see through a glass, darkly; but then face to face: now I know in part; but then shall I know even as also I am known.

[13] And now abideth faith, hope, love, these three; but the greatest of these is love.

"As for me and my house we will serve the Lord."
The Legacy Lives On

... James and John (the sons of Zebedee, but Jesus nicknamed them "Sons of Thunder"), (Mark 3:17 NLT)

Sons of Thunder

Back then, as young people, AD and I weren't so much concerned about spiritual things as we were with our childhood dreams of finishing college and maybe starting careers before marriage. It didn't work out that way, though. AD and I were married as teenagers, and we started our young family. We had to put away childhood hopes and embark on a journey of joy, pain, struggle and victory. There would be five children born of our loving union; Alveda Celeste; Alfred, II; Derek Barber; Esther Darlene and Vernon Christopher.

AD and I were the first to marry in our generation of the King Family Legacy. A few years later, when ML married Coretta, I, an only child raised by a single mother, became part of a growing family. Since my father had left my mother and me before I was born and I had never known him, Daddy King became that father to me. He was true to his word, "Better to me than my natural father could ever be."

Because we were so busy raising our young family, with AD working to finish college, we didn't immediately join the blossoming "Civil Rights Movement" of our times. AD wanted to become a "businessman." He had dreams of starting his own business.

During those days, ML graduated from college and grad school. He brought home his young and beautiful bride,

Coretta Scott King. Like me, Coretta had been born in Alabama. Coretta and I had a "striking resemblance" as young women. We were the same height, had very similar figures and dress sizes, and shiny long black hair. It has been said that AD and ML were so close that they wanted to marry women who looked alike so that their children would look alike. Whether these devoted brothers planned this or not, it turns out that Coretta and I had children who deeply resembled each other as cousins.

Somewhere along the way, AD gave up his dreams of business. I can remember when AD curtailed his dreams of entrepreneurship and accepted the call of God on his life. One day, at home in the Birth Home on Auburn Avenue, AD began acting very strangely. He was having a two-way conversation with an invisible source. He was saying things like, "Yes, what is it you want me to do? I'll do it. I hear you." I was very concerned because I couldn't get him to stop or to explain who he was talking to. I called Daddy King and expressed my concern. Dad said, "Don't worry, Baby. He's just answering the call." Later, when I read the story of the prophet Samuel, who heard someone calling him in the night, and he finally understood it was the Lord, I began to understand what happened to my husband. Although he would have been a very successful business man, God had other plans for him.

It is no coincidence that AD followed ML into ministry. With both sons following Daddy King as preachers, life began to rush forward with a building momentum, a cry for freedom. AD and ML became known as "The Sons of Thunder," after the Bible heroes James and John, known for their fiery preaching. Some say that "if ML and AD were the sons, then Daddy King must have been the thunder."

I had my first child, Alveda King, in 1951. Alveda was born while AD and I were living in the birth home on Auburn Ave. She became the very first grandchild of Daddy King and Mama King. We all knew that this was a special birth because Daddy King would often speak of how he had seen Alveda in a dream three years before she was born; and he said that she would bless many people.

Alveda was followed by Alfred Daniel King in 1952; and Derek King in 1954. Our next child, my precious Esther Darlene King was born in 1956, at the dawning of the new Civil Rights Movement. By the time our youngest, Vernon Christopher King was born in 1960, AD was caught up in the momentum of the Movement now led by his brother, Dr. Martin Luther King, Jr. By then AD had been preaching for several years.

In 1960, when Christine knew that she was to be married to Isaac Farris, she asked her beloved brothers ML and AD to officiate the ceremony. They were both ordained preachers of the Gospel of Good News for Jesus Christ, and they each loved and served humanity with happy hearts. They were agents of change in history. Divine power strengthened them to always be there for each other during that season. They graciously accepted. It was a spectacular occasion!

By that time ML had become a symbol of the struggle and AD was always close by him, encouraging him and helping him to stay strong. AD was ML's best friend, brother, and faithful strategist. The beautiful wedding was a symbol of their relationship. The wedding was witnessed by hundreds, and only helped to highlight the strength and power of these two amazing men. In the midst of guns, and dogs, and bombs and terror, the whole King family celebrated and rejoiced in the moment as the new family began their lives together.

I was pregnant with Vernon, who was born just weeks after the wedding. It truly was a romantic season, as our family always enjoyed weddings. Coretta was also pregnant with Dexter at the time, and she was barely able to fit into her bridesmaid dress. I wasn't able to march in the wedding party, with Vernon being so close to birth. The King family was increasing as the tension of the Movement was mounting.

During these years, AD loved ML so much and believed in his dreams; so many of which were his own. He did whatever he could to help him to be who he needed to become, and fully supported him. There was no jealousy and they complemented each other well. They were each other's trusted confidants. Whenever ML could not make an appointment he would send AD in his stead. It never mattered to AD; whatever ML needed, or wherever ML asked AD to go, AD did it. Cheerfully!

They were brothers committed to the same dream, the same struggle and the same mission. They strove to eliminate the three evils of war, poverty, and racism. It would become ML's and AD's destinies to preach and march in the crosshairs of danger and hate, under death threats and police surveillance. They fought for justice, equality, and freedom. These were the ultimate goals.

I was settling into my role as a pastor's wife, having supported my husband as the first lady at the Vernon Baptist Church in Newman in 1957 and at 1st Baptist Church, Ensley in Birmingham, Alabama from 1961 to 1965. From there we moved on to Zion Baptist Church in Louisville, Kentucky. I loved being a part of the different communities, doing my part to push the Civil Rights Movement forward. Over the next several years, Mama and Daddy King attended every installation service for my husband's ministries. Daddy King was very proud that his sons were preachers.

My life as AD's wife; mother of our children; and first lady was always challenging, interesting, and motivating. Even though my college matriculation ended, as did my plans to be a French major and an interior decorator, I had few regrets. AD was a strong protector and provider. He sheltered me, pampered me and loved me. We always had the very best of everything. Even though the early days of our lives were clouded with segregation, we enjoyed vacations, movies, fellowship with friends, and house parties. When AD and his siblings were growing up, their parents took them to wonderful places. They believed in living well. This part of the legacy has been passed on down to every generation. In living to serve God and bless others, we are also blessed.

Having lived in very modest circumstances for the first years of my life, I had to learn how to appreciate the blessings that surrounded AD and his family. Somewhere between living a life of faith and expecting God to bless them, while fighting the injustices of their time, they found a balance that I didn't understand at first.

They had encounters with racism; yet Daddy King always taught them that they didn't have to be treated as second-class citizens. Dad was slow to take a back seat, and would often refuse to do business in racist situations. He was a man not only concerned with the outward image, but with the inner strength and character for which his son ML would one day be renowned.

Daddy King was a polished, handsome man. Though he, too, sprang from humble beginnings, having been raised by his parents who were poor sharecroppers, he was well read, well learned, and he feared God. His sons were very handsome and polished as well. They had strength and compassion. They were the "cream of the crop."

In great part, their mother Alberta was responsible for teaching them about love and compassion. Their great-grandmother Jennie taught them to think, and to develop keen vocabularies. The three siblings had the best of everything. They lived in a beautiful home, full of luxuries that many blacks were not exposed to in those days. They read and traveled, and listened to fine music. They had tutors for music, languages, history and the arts. They dined on fine china. They wore the best clothes.

People still talk today about how Alberta King rode to school in a chauffeured limousine when she was a young girl. She was the only child of a very affluent family. She maintained that fine lifestyle throughout life. Of course, when she married a preacher, things toned down a bit. Still, Alberta, Dad's "Honey Bunch", insisted that her husband and children should enjoy life. They had beautiful cars. The Kings were well exposed to the best in life. They made sound investments in the business world. They were talented people. They were frugal and good stewards. They were generous to a fault, and supported charities and the church. Daddy and Mama King instilled these values in their children, and the legacy continues.

It was Mama King who taught me the fine art of being a lady and a pastor's wife. As the years went by, my dear husband was invited to pastor four unforgettable congregations: Mount Vernon Baptist Church in Newnan, Georgia; First Baptist Church, Ensley in Birmingham, Alabama; Zion Baptist Church in Louisville, Kentucky; and finally Ebenezer Baptist Church as co-pastor after the death of his dear brother, ML. I was there by his side as his loving helpmate.

During his life, in its many facets and phases, AD formed lasting friendships, among them brothers of the cloth. Rev. B. J. his "best friend," is godfather to our son,

Vernon. There was also Andrew Young, Joe Boone, E. H. Dorsey, Carl Moncrief, Nelson Smith, John Porter, Rev. Kirby, Otis Moss, Leo Lesser, Earskine Lewis, Dick Gregory, Georgia Davis, Lukie Ward, Aretha Franklin, Cassius Clay (Muhammad Ali), his "Ace" Fred Bennett, Sunshine, Bernard Lee, Hosea Williams, and many more. It was an honor to get to know my husband's friends. I can remember cooking meals for many of them, listening to their strategies while they shared those meals.

I realize now that it was not by accident that my mother named me Naomi Ruth. Ruth became the wife of the "Kinsman Redeemer" Boaz, and Naomi became the great-grandmother of King David, a "man after God's own heart," who was one of the greatest kings in history. I didn't know it back then, but I had become the wife of a noble "King," and become a part of a unique legacy that would one day be considered royal by many.

Through the years, as long as they lived, Daddy King and Mama King treated me as a daughter; not just as a daughter-in-law, but as their own daughter. Destiny would take me through a wonderful, unforgettable, unique, selfless, and an eventful journey; one that would require a life committed to love.

I am thankful to God for allowing me to witness and to be a part of a spiritual movement coupled with a family that would change the world using the weapons of love, compassion, peace, and non- violent social change as strategies for a way of life.

Soon I would begin to understand why I, Naomi Ruth Barber King, was destined to become a part of the now historic King Family Legacy. These two names, Naomi and Ruth, honor two of the most important women in the Bible. Naomi is remembered for her faith; and Ruth for her obedience and devotion. I didn't know it back then, but to be the wife of AD King and a member of his family would always require a tremendous amount of faith, love and obedience to the will of God. That is how I became his Ruth, and he my Boaz.

A friend loves at all times, and a brother is born for adversity." (Proverbs 17:17 KJV)

Rev. Andrew Young, Rev. AD King, Dr. ML King, Rev. Willie Bolden leading March

"So Joshua ascended from Gilgal, he, and all the people of war with him, and all the mighty men of valor. Joshua 10:7

Rev. Nelson Smith, Rev. John Porter and Rev. AD King leading march in Birmingham, AL

"Pray without ceasing." 1 Thessalonians 5:17

Rev. AD King leading prayer before a March

The 1963 Bombing of the Church Parsonage

"To come into a man's home, bomb that home, threaten the lives of his family:
What kind of people would do a thing like this?"

Rev. A D King and Mrs. Naomi King in the living room of their home after the bombing

"And Moses said unto them, 'if the children of Gad and the children of Reuben will pass with you over Jordan, every man armed to battle, before the Lord, and the land shall be subdued before you…'"
Numbers 32:29

KENTUCKY BECAME THE FIRST STATE SOUTH OF THE OHIO RIVER to enact a broad coverage civil rights law on January 27, 1966 when Governor Breathitt signed the 1966 Civil Rights Act. Robert Estill, chairman of the Kentucky Commission on Human Rights (far left) and A.D. Williams King participated in the ceremony, which was held at the base of a statue of Kentucky-born President Abraham Lincoln in the Capitol Rotunda.

"And the king said unto his servants, Know ye not that
there is a prince and
a great man fallen this day in Israel?"
2 Samuel 3:38

Jerry and Alveda's Wedding, July 1969
One week before AD's death

Brothers in the Struggle: Precious Memories

There is an old saying, "Keep your friends close, and your enemies closer." AD and ML were friends; they were even closer than many brothers ever get to become. Both men were born for adversity, and one day, they would finally pay the ultimate price for dreaming higher than most people even imagine. They laughed together, they played together. They cried together, they prayed together and they rejoiced together.

ML was a very loving, kind, spiritual, funny, and gifted person. It was fun to be around him. He and AD had grown up practicing the art of delivering sermons in the manner their father taught them. Over the years, they perfected their own unique preaching styles. I enjoyed watching them and listening to their sermons and all of their lively discussions.

Both ML and AD were electrifying preachers with different yet very effective deliveries. They had a way of reaching and capturing the essence of the moment. They made you want to stop and listen and their words made you want to go out immediately and be active in changing the world we lived in, while ultimately seeking a permanent eternal reward. More than anything, they wanted life to be better; to be abundantly just and fair. We learned to believe, because they did.

Unforgettable moments with my brother-in-law MLK

After the birth of Yolanda King in 1955, I went to spend time with Coretta. My niece, Yolanda, was both on my birthday; November 17, 1955. I was born the same day in 1931.

One night, ML came in and it was very late and dark. I was sitting in the living room. ML came in and walked to the mantle in the living room. He could not see my face because of the darkness. As he walked to the mantle, he was tugging on his tie and adjusting it. Then he turned to me and said, "Neenie, do you know what happened to me today?" And I asked curiously, "What, ML?" He then told me he was detained at the police station and that they had tried to choke him with his own tie. He then said, "Neenie, you know, the more they try to abuse us, the more we are going to forgive and love them."

Here was this man whom I loved and respected so much, now fighting bullies who wore police badges that held all the power and hated him only because of the color of his skin. In that moment I knew what true bravery was. And almost immediately tears began rolling endlessly down my face, because I knew that he had been chosen by God to lead the Civil Rights Movement just as Moses led the Israelites out of peril in Egypt. He was without question prepared for the cause—or rather, the war—for equality, justice, and freedom for his people.

And I loved him so, because I knew some times he must have wanted to stoop to their level and repay evil with evil—but he never did. He chose to fight with intelligence. He armed himself with knowledge and used his words as his most powerful weapon. He taught me that there was a better way to fight, and he illuminated the way.

Danger in New York.

ML was in New York City autographing his first book entitled, "*Strides Toward Freedom*" when a demented woman approached him and suddenly asked, "Are you Martin Luther King, Jr.?" He simply responded, "Yes." The next thing he knew she was stabbing him in the chest with a very sharp knife. It seemed the more he fought for peace, the less he received. People seemed intent on stopping him from fulfilling his destiny.

The tip of the blade was very close to his main artery. Had the blade punctured his vein, he would have bled to death. He was realizing that people would repay his nonviolence with even more violence. It was a very frightening experience for him. But it only made him stronger.

ML wrote a speech about his experience entitled, "If I Had Sneezed." The main story of the piece was about a little white girl who wrote a letter to him and told him that she was glad that he did not sneeze—because if he had sneezed at that moment, he would have died!

When I watched the news on the television, I called the hospital to express my well wishes and asked ML if there was anything I could do to help make him feel better. ML replied easily, "Make me a sweet potato pie." I laughed happily in the knowledge that he was stronger than any of us realized, and I called Coretta to find out when she would be travelling to New York to see him. I prepared the sweet potato pie with love and placed it in a container. I ensured it was freshly prepared, warm, wrapped, and delivered to Coretta for ML. Upon Coretta's arrival at the hospital, she called me and handed the phone to ML. I then asked again how he was feeling, and he responded by saying that he felt much better now that he was eating the sweet potato pie! These were wonderful moments in history, and wonderful moments of my life.

ML and AD in Birmingham, AL

The story of Birmingham would not be complete without recalling the role AD played. AD became the leader of the movement and gathered together with Shuttlesworth, Rev. Nelson, Rev. Smith and many others. AD's congregation in Ensley, AL (located on the outskirt of Birmingham) was the largest and had the greatest audience to influence. He played a significant role in Birmingham's history as he shaped the strategy of the movement, which required a myriad of great thinkers and doers—and AD was both. When people were arrested for peacefully protesting the injustice they faced, they were required to pay bail for their release and it had an economic impact on the movement. AD King knew the community, and would help raise money to free those detained.

However, he felt that the movement strategy was not effective enough. He wanted to do something revolutionary that he knew would change the image of those who were fighting. He then introduced the strategy of putting the children in front of the line starting with his own 5 little children. Although he must have been terribly afraid that these people filled with hatred would hurt his beloved children, I think he knew deep inside that God would protect them and allow them to have a voice to scream out against the world which judged them solely on the color of their skin.

Congregation in Birmingham

AD King's church members saw his children in front of the line and responded by joining the demonstration with their children. The movement changed in size to the extent that the police could not arrest all of them at once; therefore, they had to lock them up in the stadium. AD converted the stadium into a revival! He turned all of the negative, hateful energy and used it to fuel a passion in the people that was electrifying! AD introduced this strategy all over the south. The movement became a thorn in the flesh of the oppressors that expressed themselves as the police.

At this time AD had begun to get a lot of negative attention from the bullying system around him. On May 11, 1963 Rev. AD King's house was bombed. Half of the house was completely destroyed, and the family escaped through the back door and over the fence to safety. Had it not been for God that night we would have all perished! I'm convinced without a shadow of doubt that God ushered my husband into the living room to come and check on me. He held my hand sweetly and said quietly, "Naomi, it is a little too quiet, you could hear a cotton ball fall." He pulled me from where I sat and started to move me away from the windows. By the time we got to the middle of the house the second bomb went off, and in seconds most of our home was gone. Coincidentally, ML had left the same study room a day before the bombing to move to the motel which was also bombed that same night. Fortunately for all of us, ML had already left the motel and was headed on his way to Atlanta.

At the height of this atrocity, the house of a prominent lawyer was also bombed there in Birmingham. Rev. AD King bravely stood on the hood of a car with a bull horn and said to a tense crowd, "We have had a difficult night; if you are going to kill someone, then kill me…. But Stand Up for Justice, Stand Up for Equality, Stand Up for Freedom and Stand Up for your Rights! But with NON VIOLENCE!" He refused to stoop to the level of those who thought they could forcibly shut him up for good.

When I now see the picture of my living room where I was sitting before my husband came in and took my hand, I am reminded of God's grace. I could have been killed. God spared my life—all of our lives—as I could have been killed or seriously injured by the bomb. I am reminded every day by that picture, of the grace of God and the purpose of God for my life. When God visits you, He gives you courage, hope, and the strength to do His will.

Selma Demonstration.

The bombing of the 16th Street church killed four little girls whose only crime had been serving the Lord. This event in particular, coupled with the bombing of AD King's house and many others, the demonstrations in Birmingham, and a multitude of other factors led Congress to pass the Civil Rights Acts of 1964. What a great period in history: a period of pain, a period of bravery, and most importantly, a period of change. Ensley Park erected a statue of the following three pastors kneeling down praying: Reverend A.D King, Reverend Nelson and Reverend Smith. This statue served as a reminder of the struggle for equality, justice and freedom.

Selma, Alabama

The fight for equality, justice and freedom became everyone's focus and there was no turning back. There was no longer a fear of man nor woman, and it didn't matter the color of their skin. The momentum only grew and became stronger with the power of non- violence, prayer, courage and determination. It became the people's movement; black and white together fighting for justice, equality, and freedom. They knew that things were changing, but they knew they still had a long way to go before the change they sought would come.

AD King was the chairman of the Kentucky Christian Leadership Conference and one of the lead directors of the Southern Christian Leadership Conference. ML was the president of the SCLC and the leader of the movement. AD and ML kept in contact every single day, strategizing and planning together. After much deliberation, AD decided to lease a plane from Perdue University and fly them from Louisville, Kentucky to Selma, Alabama. The group was diverse and that gave much credence to the struggle. AD knew how to mobilize young people. He knew how to rally children and to get them to see their vital role in the struggle. ML depended on him so much. The infamous march to Selma is known as Bloody Sunday. The police brutality was at its highest and there seemed to be no shame for their unwarranted violence. AD was wounded and John Lewis was seriously injured, and so many more civil rights leaders were hospitalized as a result of the demonstration and the atrocities that were committed by the police. ML was pushed into the car and driven to safety. More than anything at this time, we needed to keep him safe. Both brothers played significant roles in the struggle side by side.

As a result of the Selma demonstration, the Voting Right Act of 1965 was passed by Congress. This law paved the way for the election of an African American President of the United States, a historic landmark, erected on the shoulders of many giants of history who sacrificed their very lives for a better America, and a better world.

There are no streets named after Reverend AD King and no statues—but history will never forget him, because he did not die in vain. There were two brothers with the same dream, the same commitment, and the same struggle. They were blood brothers from the same lineage. They were close in life and could not even be separated by death.

The Selma demonstration brought so much pain and sorrow that only time would heal. A brave 39 year-old mother of five children who stood beside AD and ML and the magnificent movement was murdered in cold blood for her undeniable passion for justice, fairness and freedom for all of God's children, a woman of unprecedented commitment. Her name was Viola Liuzzo.

According to AD, Viola was a brave woman of vigor who was fearless, courageous and selfless. She happened to be a white woman, but gave her life to the movement in spite of the known danger of the times. She will never be forgotten as a mother of the Civil Rights Movement and a devoted icon of the 21st century. May her departed soul rest in perfect peace.

AD remembered other notable people who answered the call for justice across the spectrum of America including many Jews led by Rabbi Abraham Joshua Heschel. We owe them a great gratitude and we are better off for their sacrifice and commitment to justice, fairness and freedom.

Rev. James Orange was recruited by Rev. AD King and became a foot soldier of the Civil Rights Movement for many decades. He also fought for the dismantling of white rule in South Africa which led to the freedom of Nelson

Mandela who became the first black President of South Africa.

Open Housing in Louisville, Kentucky

AD King was fearless, courageous and committed to non-violent strategies as a way of life. He organized many demonstrations in Louisville, Kentucky. He became a pastor at Zion Baptist Church in 1965. He formed the Kentucky Christian Leadership Conference and maintained the title of chairman of the organization from 1965-1968. He used the organization as a base for dismantling segregation, and for the housing accommodation known as open housing.

In simple terms, open housing ordinances were aimed at changing laws that banned African Americans from buying homes in certain areas of the community by virtue of their skin color and ethnicity. AD used the same strategy he had used in Birmingham to fight his battles in Louisville by magnificently mobilizing young people. He set up voter registration centers and organized campaign strategies. In 1968 the Open Housing Ordinance was passed into law in the state of Kentucky, and the pen the governor used to sign the law was given to AD King as a gesture of good will. As a result of this demonstration, the first black senator was elected by the name of Senator Georgia Powers. This is another testimony to the success of the struggle.

AD King made a mark on history. And because of that, he paid dearly for his role in the demonstrations. He sustained an injury to his left eye when a stone was thrown in his direction. The target was meant for ML, but AD shielded his brother and instead was struck. He didn't mind. Fighting for his brother had now become a way of life. He was a thorn in the flesh of the system that created and sustained hatred for the people of color and as a result, Zion Baptist church in Louisville was bombed. It was clear that the oppressors would do whatever they could to silence those who rose against them.

ML and AD in Memphis, Last Journey

Rev AD King and his brother ML were both staying at the Lorraine Hotel. AD King was in room 206 while his brother ML was right above him in room 306. Earlier that day, they had strategized and planned the rally for the sanitation workers who were marginalized and poorly treated.

ML held a meeting in AD's room with the other SCLC members, and at the end of the meeting they were all in good spirits. AD and ML even playfully started a pillow fight with Andrew Young joining in. Shortly afterward, ML asked AD if he would like to go to dinner at Reverend Kyle's house. It was a rare occasion, but AD declined and told ML to go on ahead and have a nice dinner. AD needed some rest after making the drive from Louisville to Memphis.

Shockingly, Reverend AD was awakened from his sleep and given the news that his brother had been fatally wounded… killed. He was beyond devastated and blamed himself for resting peacefully in his bed and not protecting his brother when he had needed him the most. He felt that if he had agreed to go to dinner, his brother would still be alive. He wept day in and day out furiously. They had taken the light out of his life, and out of the Civil Rights Movement. AD never recovered from the loss of his brother.

ML's Funeral

ML's body was flown from Memphis to Atlanta for burial. AD accompanied the police to ensure that his brother was treated with the upmost respect and dignity. AD cried openly at the burial. He would never be the same again after he lost his brother. And neither would the world.

Historic Ebenezer Baptist Church

After the assassination of ML, AD became co-pastor with his father. The position was once held by ML. He transformed the church in honor of his brother and founded the children's chapel, which was televised on Channel 5 for about 25 years after his death on July 21, 1969.

Last Sermons

The last two sermons preached by AD were centered on the "Woman with the Issue of Blood," and discovering how to say and live the truth of "Peace is Still", as he marveled at the authority and power of the living God.

Death

AD King was martyred on July 21, 1969, fifteen months after his famous brother was killed.

AD led demonstrations in Florida, Memphis, social circles in Georgia, and many other places. He did not venture to take the reins of leadership from Rev. Ralph Abernathy, the president of SCLC, but supported him as he had supported his brother. He made the pronouncement after his brother's death that ML had decided that in the case of his eventual death that Rev. Ralph Abernathy should be installed as the new president of the SCLC. On the day of his martyrdom Al II had driven AD to church. Naomi was in Jamaica with Mrs. Coretta Scott King and Vernon King.

On that night, around midnight—AD, Alveda, and Derek sang happy birthday to Al. His birthday was July 21. After the singing of the birthday song, they prayed and AD asked the children to go to bed in order to prepare for Al's driving test the next morning. Just before they went to bed, Reverend King was speaking on the phone. He became so agitated that his children began asking him what was wrong. They overheard AD saying with much emotion, "I'm going to find out who killed my brother and you can count on that! I will not rest until I find who killed my brother." When Alveda inquired from her father who the caller was, Rev. King simply replied, "Do not worry, it was just a prank call." Alveda and her husband Jerry were newlyweds. They were just returning from their brief honeymoon, having been married the weekend before.

They retired to bed along with her brothers, because she and Jerry had to go to work the next morning.

Later, Reverend B.J. Johnson was on the phone with Reverend AD until around 1:30 am. Reverend King told Reverend Johnson, "Good night."

Reverend AD King's body was found in the family's pool early the next morning. His body was discovered by his son Derek. He immediately called Alveda at work. "Daddy is in the pool. He is dead." Alveda immediately ran to her supervisor, and African American man who drove her home so fast that they arrived just after the ambulance and police appeared on the scene.

When the body was pulled out of the swimming pool a paramedic tried a compression technique and found there to be no water in his lungs, which meant that he was dead before he had ever hit the water. Witnesses at the scene even reported him saying: "There's no water in his lungs. He was dead when he hit the water!"

I believe that my husband was killed. Many others have come to the same conclusion. When I examined his body at the mortuary before he was released for burial, I clearly saw that he had rings around his neck and bruises on his head and stomach. He was found in the fetal position at the bottom of the pool with no water in his lungs. I am convinced that he was murdered because they could not stand living with the power of two Kings, ML and AD walking this earth; dreaming the same dream; demanding the freedom that didn't just belong to them—it belonged to us all.

In a way they were like the Kennedy brothers – killed for having the same dream.

AD and ML fought for you and for me. They helped to destroy a system of bullying that was so strong, it had seemed unbreakable for so long. But nothing was too hard for these brave men and women. They were, and will forever be, legendary. I am blessed to have known them and shared so many beautiful memories with both AD and ML. It was truly an honor.

As the "old folks" say: "May their souls rest in perfect peace." I shall never forget ML and AD and neither will the world. I loved my husband dearly, and I could never repay him for what he did for me and our children, but I can thank him for what he did for the world. "Thank You AD, for your tireless dedication and service to all of us who rode your waves to freedom. We didn't all make it to the "Promised Land" together, but because you and your brother shared a dream —we realize more of it each day."

Afterword

People always remark that my sister-in-law, Coretta, and I look alike. AD used to laugh about how he and ML as young boys had always said that they would marry women who looked alike—with long hair, little waists, and big legs. I suppose that Coretta and I would have fit those descriptions as brides. What is remarkable is the similarity in resemblance among our children, even though they are cousins rather than siblings. It makes a good conversation piece. People remark about the resemblances all the time.

AD and ML were preachers, following after their father, grandfather, and Uncle Joel. As young men, prior to their ordinations, they used to have "whooping" contests, competing with their homiletics to such an extent that they would draw a crowd. What a sight to behold!

After they accepted their respective pastorates, they would visit each other, and preach in each other's pulpits. They were remarkable preachers, full of fire and truth. They both loved the Bible, and delighted in preaching the gospel.

AD and ML were also partners in the Civil Rights Movement. When ML marched, AD was often there at his side. In Birmingham, Louisville, and other cities, ML relied on AD for strategy, organization, and leadership. They were often praised and maligned as well. They were lauded and ostracized. In most cities, they were either received as heroes or called "rabble rousers and outside agitators." What many don't remember is that many blacks as well as whites resented ML's going against the status-quo. People were generally comfortable with racism, and if not comfortable, they adapted. Few wanted to rock the boat, so to speak.

For the most part, I lived in the background. I do remember one occasion where I was riding on a city bus, alone. My husband and children were not with me. This was before Rosa Parks and Montgomery. When I got on the bus, I refused to go and sit in the back. I knew that I was a human being, and should be treated with dignity. The bus driver stopped the bus and said that he would "kill my black a--" if I didn't either go to the back of the bus or get off. For a moment, I started to rebel, and then remembered my precious, beautiful family waiting for me at home. I stared at the bus driver without a word and got off the bus. Needless to say, I was a major supporter of Rosa Parks when she made her monumental decision to keep her seat and her dignity.

Still, for the most part, my husband and I agreed that if our children were to have any sense of stability, it would be good for me to remain in the home, and allow him to go to the front of the battlefield. Together, we instilled in our children the same values of freedom, equality and human compassion that he and ML espoused from their pulpits and picket lines—back when America grappled with her social conscience and searched for her soul. I believed that we were a team, me at home and him out in the streets. AD was free to support his brother, as he had done all of his life. For all of the years of the Movement, AD was there for ML, and more often with him.

AD was there in Memphis when ML was shot. He had gone there the night before to "help my brother," he said as he left home.

When ML died, AD was heartbroken. He would sit quietly at night, and cry because he felt so alone. He was forever grieved, because he loved his brother so very much. AD was a man of compassion who loved with a passion for life and humanity. The loss of his brother was devastating.

Even though I have missed my husband sorely, I often wonder how he would have taken the deaths of his mother, Alberta, and our three children, Alfred, Darlene and Vernon. Mama King was shot in the tragic incident at Ebenezer, and Alfred and Darlene died in separate jogging incidents. Each of these incidents took a heavy toll in my life. I have often cried because AD wasn't there to help me through it, while at the same time I was glad that he didn't have to be here to suffer the pain. What a paradox.

When Mama King was shot while playing the organ at Ebenezer, I was there in the congregation. When the ambulance came, God somehow allowed me to be the only person to ride in the vehicle with her. I believe I heard her last breath; a sigh as she touched her cheek where she had been wounded. For those last moments, it was Mama King, Jesus, and me. I will never forget it.

On the way to the hospital, my eyes remained fixed on her. She gasped one time, and pressed her hand to her face where one bullet had penetrated. Although they worked on her for quite a while in the emergency room, I believe Mama King died in the ambulance when she gasped that one last time. This was such a tremendous loss. The pain was unbearable. At that time, I never imagined that we would all have to suffer even more tragedy.

The drama would continue to unfold. My precious children, Darlene and Alfred, died while running on the track. Darlene was there for exercise. A few years later, Alfred, a sports buff, was working out. A lady who passed him by while he was lying on the ground looking up at the sky before his last fatal lap paused to ask him what he was thinking about. She later told us that he said, "I'm asking God to help these tired old legs make it around just one more time."

Al was in his mid-thirties, yet he was tired. I have often believed that the stress of the Civil Rights Movement and the burdens we were all required to bear were just too much for all of my precious dear ones. AD, ML, my dear mother Bessie, Mama King, Darlene, and Al—how much I miss them. I miss Daddy King, too. His passing was the only death not linked to tragedy. Yet, he was sad at the end as well.

Yet, all was never lost, and there were joyful moments always mixed in with the sorrow. AD and ML understood this until the very last moments of their lives. They lived their lives to the fullest. To say that ML and AD were close would be such an understatement. Their lives were so parallel in so many ways. They looked alike as well. AD was taller, and had a deeper voice. His skin tone was fair; ML's a richer brown. AD was a practical joker, but both men shared a delightful sense of humor; they made jokes all the time. Like AD, ML loved my cooking, and would visit us often before he was married to Coretta.

Coretta was a good cook as well, and was a lovely hostess throughout her marriage to ML. All of the women in our family have been good cooks and lovely homemakers throughout the generations. We are known for our gracious hospitality, our love of beauty, and our fierce regard for our children and family members.

Yet, the times of peril were so real, and if God had not been with us every step of the way, I guess we would have been frightened to death. Even in the height of the death threats against his life and the threats to his family, AD shielded us as much as he could. He was a buffer through the storms.

My husband was a wonderful leader and organizer. People flocked to him during the days of the Movement. He was a people's man. Everybody loved my husband. He was charming, vibrant, and full of life. He kept us all so secure in his circle of love and protection that I am still thankful that I didn't have to face some of the horrors of the time. I know that AD's strength came from God. I am just so thankful that God sustained us.

My husband's death was a tragedy unto itself. He died on our son Alfred's sixteenth birthday. He was found in our pool at home, with a bruise on his head and with no water in his lungs. I was out of the country at the time. When I arrived back in Atlanta and went to view his body, there were bruises on his neck and upper torso. Reports from the rescue team, witnessed by bystanders, said that "there was no water in his lungs. He was dead when he hit the water." Efforts to retrieve medical reports proved fruitless because we were constantly told that the records were lost, or had never been recorded.

There had been several attempts on my husband's life, prior to his death. Our home and church had been bombed. We lived under the constant threats that were so prevalent to many of that era. Daddy King continued to say until his death, "They killed my boys." He was convinced that both sons had fallen as victims, martyrs of an era of violence and hope.

AD has been gone many years now. He never knew our grandchildren and great-grandchildren. This book is a gift to them and to the world. I like to believe that AD and ML are in Heaven together now. They know only joy, and it becomes a comfort to remember them with joy.

"Therefore, if anyone is in Christ, he is a new creation. The old has passed away; behold, the new has come."
2 Corinthians 5:17

Mrs. Naomi Ruth Barber King
"The Butterfly Queen"

About the Author

Born in Dothan, Alabama in 1932, Mrs. Naomi Ruth Barber King was destined to become a woman of quiet dignity, strength and support to her husband, her family and the communities around her. Naomi would come to walk in the grace and distinction of her beloved butterflies, and acquire the noted title of the "Butterfly Queen."

Like the butterfly, Mrs. King brings beauty and joy to everyone around her. Colorful and talented, she uses her creativity to handle the most difficult tasks, and manages to put those near her at ease in the process. "Jesus is my anchor, and I praise God for His love and blessings," she often proclaims.

She leads a life of grace and compassion in a world where unsung heroines go unnoticed by many, while touching lives and changing hearts in the highways and byways of communities in need of love. Born on November 17, 1931 to a single mother, Bessie Barber Bailey, Naomi was raised as "an only child" in a sheltered and protected environment. Naomi's mother was a domestic worker who gave her daughter the best available in the form of nurture, clothing, education and spiritual development. "Mama" Bessie was a favored cook in a prominent Atlanta home. They had moved to Atlanta to "make a better living" for themselves. "Mama Bessie" spared nothing for the upbringing of her daughter. Thanks to the generosity of her mother's employers, Naomi wore the finest clothes, observed the most admired social graces and received the best education possible for her times.

Bessie and Naomi joined Ebenezer Baptist Church and began to grow spiritually under the pastorate of Rev. ML Luther King, Sr. and his wife, Mrs. Alberta Williams King. Naomi got to know their children, and caught the eye of their youngest son, AD King who would become her "Boaz."

As a young woman, Naomi was charming, graceful, willowy and beautiful. She stood out in a crowd, and was often selected by local clothing stores as a preferred fashion model, earning for her the distinct honor of being featured in shop windows and circulars right along with "white" counterparts. Later, photographs of Naomi and her children would also appear in prominent Atlanta photographers' galleries.

Naomi was educated in Atlanta public schools. She was a notable student, winning awards for writing and music. She was active in church and community projects, and was popular and respected by her peers. She also worked part time as a print and runway model. Naomi attended Spelman College in Atlanta, GA for one year prior to her marriage to AD Williams King Sr. – youngest son of Martin Luther, King Sr. and Alberta King. She later attended the University of Alabama where she studied interior design.

She excelled in French and English. Her scholastic abilities, especially her writing skills earned for her the distinct opportunity to address her class at her high school graduation. Her extracurricular talents included writing poetry, dancing and singing. She entered college as a "French Major." Parlez-vous?

During their marriage, AD accepted "the call" to ministry, following in the footsteps of his great-grandfather and slave preacher, Rev. Willis Williams; his grandfather, Rev. Dr. AD Williams; his father, Dr. Martin Luther King, Sr., and his brother, Dr. Martin Luther King, Jr.

As the wife of a prominent minister, who promptly joined his brother in the Civil Rights Struggle, Naomi blossomed as a mother of five. She advanced in her ministry as first lady of the prominent churches, Mt. Vernon First Baptist Church in Newnan, GA; First Baptist Church Ensley, Birmingham, ALA, Zion Baptist Church in Louisville, KY, and Ebenezer Baptists Church in Atlanta, GA, where her husband ministered during his lifetime.

Naomi considers her ultimate calling was always that of wife, mother, and First Lady. With the support and guidance of "Daddy King," she married AD and they began their family. They would parent five children, and together become the "quiet support" of Dr. Martin Luther King, Jr.; a leader of the Civil Rights Movement of the 20th Century.

Naomi recalls that her courtship and marriage to Rev. King is a wonderful "love story." AD called her "Neenie." As the young wife of her activist husband, Rev. AD King, II, she stood as First Lady, confidant, prayer partner and advisor to the younger brother of the more famous Dr. Martin Luther King, Jr. In the height of the civil rights battles, where together AD and Naomi lived through the bombings of their home and later their church, Naomi was a "quiet strength" to her husband and family.

During his lifetime, Rev. AD shepherded four churches. At his side, Mrs. AD Williams King stood as First Lady, bringing musical concerts, women's enrichment programs and gracious tools for living to their congregations. She was a noted hostess of women's teas and a much sought after women's day speaker.

"First Lady," as Naomi was affectionately called by the faithful flocks, assisted her husband, Dr. Alfred Daniel Williams King "first and foremost by helping to raise our children." Her mastery of the social graces cause this trend setter to be remembered and sought after for her cooking, A-1 hostess presentations, and event planning.

Along with being the anchor in the home while her husband "risked his life to fight for the freedom of the oppressed," Naomi also sang at concerts to raise funds for the "Movement," served as a "Women's Day Speaker" at churches to which she was invited, and organized "teas and prayer circle activities" which helped to stabilize the communities. AD and "Neenie" shared a life of trials and triumphs, which she fondly remembers as "a love story."

Rev. AD King was a "victim of the racism of the times. Working closely with his brother, Dr. Martin Luther

King, Jr., AD's home and church were bombed, and he experienced many death threats. His death remains an unsolved mystery." Naomi King is a consulting producer for the award winning theatrical documentary and feature film regarding the life and legacy of her heroic husband.

Her professional accomplishments include Citizens Trust Bank, Bank of Louisville, interior decorating and design, managing the King Center gift shop, and serving as a "devoted and privileged traveling companion to my sister-in-law, Mrs. Coretta Scott King." Mrs. King holds awards and special recognition, such as recipient of the S. C. L. C. Rosa Parks Award, King for America Truth Finder Award, featured in the AARP documentary "Voices of Civil Rights, and holds memberships in NAACP, SCLC, Priests for Life, Women of SCLC, SCLC Women, and American Bridge Association. She is a recognized author and is noted for her devotion to her God, her family and her church.

Today, Mrs. King is a beloved mother, grandmother, great grandmother, relative, friend, comfort and bright light to those in the church and communities she serves. Naomi is the inspiration of the documentary project AD King: Brother to the Dreamer. She is an author and speaks out on important issues of the day. For more information, please visit www.adkingfoundation.com

Appendix

Now that you have learned more about the life of AD King and how he helped his brother ML to impact the world and bring about change for good, it is important to know a tested and proven formula for implementing the process of nonviolent social change in the global society.

After the Bible, perhaps one of the most valuable guides for developing the strategies of the 20th Century Civil Rights Movement would be principles and steps towards a nonviolent way of living.

AD joined ML in making a personal and public commitment to solving the problems of their day by applying God's Word, walking in God's love and demonstrating the principles and steps of nonviolence. While ML wrote about these steps, he, his brother and indeed all of the foot soldiers of the Movement were trained in these steps and principles. It therefore seems fitting to include them in this book:

SIX PRINCIPLES FOR NONVIOLENT LIVING

Building upon the foundation for nonviolent living begins with these principles and steps:

1. Nonviolent living requires courage. It involves confronting the forces of injustice, and uses righteous

anger, prayer and the will, mind and emotions to ultimately bring about change, reconciliation and lasting transformation.
2. Attaining the reality of the Beloved Community is the quest. The desire is to attain a peaceful, reconciled existence for everyone by creating harmonious relationships where among people where true and unbiased justice prevails; thereby allowing people to attain their full potential in life.
3. Resist the forces of evil while loving the people entrapped in the evil circumstances. The nonviolent loving approach enables the practitioner to objectively examine the existing conditions, policies and practices of the conflict; and further to determine the cause of and then root out and eliminate the conflict. The practitioner of nonviolence thereby becomes proactive rather than reactive.
4. Accept any and all suffering; physical, mental, material and otherwise without striking back with fist, words or weapons. Let your weapons be love, prayer and forgiveness. Do this for the sake of achieving the common good for all. Suffering in this manner allows God to move us towards redemption; and can cause the opponent to rethink his or her position.
5. Seek freedom from violence of the spirit, soul and body. This position is a force to be reckoned with; and brings advantage to the campaign. The face of nonviolence mirrors Agape Love.
6. The Creator of the Universe stands for righteous, truth and justice together. When this is understood, then the end which leads to victory is in sight.

The Six Steps/Phases For Nonviolent Transformation include:

1. ***Gather Information*** – The way you determine the facts, the options for change, and the timing of pressure for raising the issue is a collective process.
2. ***Educate Your Community*** – The process for developing articulate leaders, who are knowledgeable about the issues. It is directed toward the community through all forms of media about the real issues and human consequences of an unjust situation.
3. ***Commit first before seeking commitment from others*** – This means looking at your internal and external involvement in the nonviolent campaign and preparing yourself for long-term as well as short-term action.
4. ***Compassionate Negotiation*** – Is the art of bringing together your views and those of your opponent to arrive at a just conclusion or clarify the unresolved issues, at which point, the conflict is formalized.
5. ***Overt Encounters*** – Should occur when negotiations have broken down or failed to produce a fair and mutually beneficial response to the contested issues and conditions.
6. ***Transformational Reconciliation*** – Is the desired conclusion to a crusade of campaign. Once faith, hope and love are genuinely applied, the opponents and proponents should look forward to a celebration of victory and be prepared to enter into a season of joint leadership to implement change and lasting transformation.

THE STRUGGLE CONTINUES...REV. A. D. KING

I dearly love the two brothers who were closer than
breathing and for them I prayed….
Naomi RuthBarber King

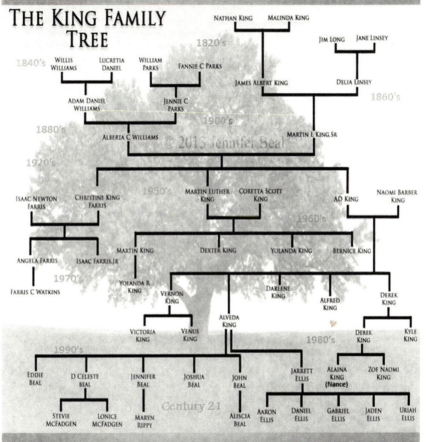

FOR GENERATIONS TO COME

By Dr. Alveda C. King

Our family tree
means more to me, Than silver
or gold, or a
Rolls Royce.

I can rejoice and be glad,
that Mother and Dad, loved each other
- and GOD
Who blessed their union.

From one to another, we are linked
to each other...
Through the blessings and mercy of our awesome
CREATOR

Our Creator, the Artist, Who reminds us of
ETERNITY

In the smiles of our children, who have the
Spirit of our ancestors-
Twinkling out from their eyes...

Reminding us
Of GENERATIONS to COME.

Notes:

Notes:

Notes:

CPSIA information can be obtained at www.ICGtesting.com
Printed in the USA
LVOW10s2234240415

436028LV00003B/3/P